WEST SUSSEX

YEAR ROUND WALKS

Spring, Summer, Autumn & Winter

David Weller

COUNTRYSIDE BOOKS

NEWBURY BERKSHIRE

First published 2012
Revised and reprinted 2018
Reprinted 2020
© David Weller 2012
Photographs by David Weller

COUNTRYSIDE BOOKS
3 Catherine Road
Newbury, Berkshire

To view our complete range of books,
please visit us at
www.countrysidebooks.co.uk

ISBN 978 1 84674 263 7

*To my lovely wife, Marilyn, for all the help and
support she gave me whilst writing this book.*

*All materials used in the manufacture of
this book carry FSC certification.*

Produced by The Letterworks Ltd., Reading
Typeset by KT Designs, St Helens
Printed by The Holywell Press, Oxford

Contents

Contents

Autumn

Winter

Introduction

Firstly I have an admission to make: I am a 'fair weather' walker. This affliction, however, has never restricted me to only walking during the summer. No, over the good many years I have enjoyed rambling through our wonderful countryside, I have found there is still so much to see during the rest of the year. We all know what summer brings for the rambler: the sweet smell of the pine forest, skylarks singing overhead and dog roses blooming in the hedgerow, but what about the rest of the year?

In spring, new life abounds as the countryside awakens from its winter slumber and trees begin to unfurl their fresh leaves; the flowers of the meadow and hedgerow begin to bloom while newborn lambs breathe their first in the fields.

Then, as summer fades into the golden glow of autumn, all that energy gained from the sun produces wonderful fruits in the hedgerow; leaves begin to fall from the trees to provide food for the next year's growth and interesting fungi shoot up from the soil to spread their spores.

Although winter days are shorter, many are bright and crisp, with a stillness in the air that offers further joys: the crunch of a hoar frost underfoot, new vistas discovered now the leaves have fallen from the trees and a much better chance to spot a deer or two.

So, if up until now you have confined your country walking to only the summer months, then I hope my little book will change that because there is so much pleasure to be gained 'off season'.

Most of the circuits I have devised for this collection of walks are suitable for any time of the year, but I have suggested a season when I personally believe they have something special to offer and for each one I have written a point of interest that you might spot along the way. Where possible, I have also suggested a place for a bite to eat near each route.

My maps are drawn to scale and contain numbers that relate to each paragraph of the walk, although I do recommend you take the relevant Ordnance Survey Explorer (1:25,000) map mentioned at the beginning of each circuit.

Please respect the countryside and don't pick any wildflowers that you see, no matter how numerous they appear; even bluebells are becoming endangered nowadays.

Happy walking, all year round!

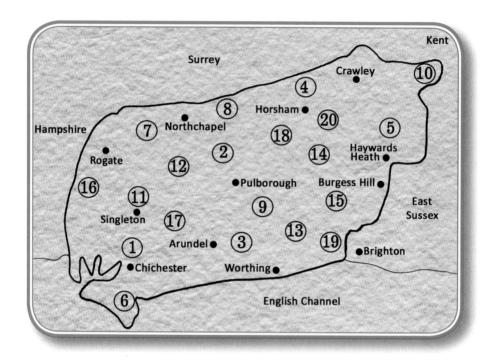

PUBLISHER'S NOTE

We hope that you obtain considerable enjoyment from this book; great care has been taken in its preparation. Although at the time of publication all routes followed public rights of way or permitted paths, diversion orders can be made and permissions withdrawn.

We cannot, of course, be held responsible for such diversion orders and any inaccuracies in the text which result from these or any other changes to the routes, nor any damage which might result from walkers trespassing on private property. We are anxious though that all details covering the walks are kept up to date and would therefore welcome information from readers which would be relevant to future editions.

The simple sketch maps that accompany the walks in this book are based on notes made by the author whilst checking out the routes on the ground. They are designed to show you how to reach the start, to point out the main features of the overall circuit and they contain a progression of numbers that relate to the paragraphs of the text.

However, for the benefit of a proper map, we do recommend that you purchase the relevant Ordnance Survey sheet covering your walk. The Ordnance Survey maps are widely available, especially through booksellers and local newsagents.

1 The Trundle, East Lavant and Haye's Down

The wonderful view from Haye's Down

This lovely circuit has extraordinary views over the surrounding countryside from almost its whole length; even from the car park! After a short climb to the crest of St Roche's Hill known as The Trundle, the route follows easily walked tracks for two miles with extensive views over Chichester and beyond before reaching its turning point in the pretty village of East Lavant. After walking the village street, the way begins its return by following a lovely track alongside a clear-running stream and through the dappled shade of woodland to reach Haye's Down. Here the route climbs the downs above a patchwork of fields where little has changed for centuries. After continuing along a slowly rising field path The Trundle is rejoined where the end of the walk awaits at the far side.

Spring

The Facts

Distance 5½ miles.

Terrain There is one hill of note at Haye's Down but it is not beyond a person of average fitness. This route is not suitable in winter or after prolonged rain.

Map OS Explorer 120 Chichester, South Harting and Selsey.

Starting point The Triangle car park in Goodwood Country Park (GR 879113).

How to get there From the A286 at Singleton, 5 miles north of Chichester, follow the signs to the Open Air Museum, pass its entrance and continue for 1¼ miles to reach the car park on your left.

Refreshments The Royal Oak pub in East Lavant. ☎ 01243 527434.

The Walk

1 From the car park, cross the road and follow a grassy path to the right of steps and climb to the crest of **The Trundle**. When opposite a radio mast, fork right and continue along a grassy cart track, passing to the left of a second mast. Continue through the still visible defensive ditch of the Iron Age fort. Keep ahead along a broad stony track to meet **Seven Points** car park.

The remains of an Iron Age fort called The Trundle are here on the summit of St Roche's Hill and the banks and ditches are still clearly visible. Latterly, a chapel and windmill existed here although both are now gone. Trundle is an Old English word for 'circle'.

2 At the far end of the car park and a junction of tracks, turn left on a downhill wide track known as **Chalkpit Lane,** with the spire of **Chichester Cathedral** in the distance. Remain on this easy-walking track now for 2 miles until it meets the village street in **East Lavant**.

3 Turn right along the street, pass by the **Royal Oak** pub and at a road junction press on ahead along **Pook Lane**. Cross the clear-running waters of the **River Lavant** from which the village is named and at a fork in the road follow the right fork along **Sheepwash Lane**.

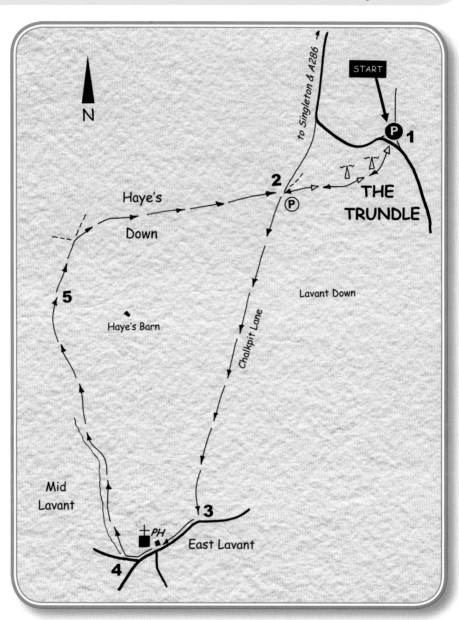

④ Look out for a bridleway signed to your right along the drive of **Staple House Farm**. Follow the drive and when it turns into the extensive grounds, maintain direction ahead on a cart track beside the **River Lavant**. Remain on this track for 1¼ miles until a gate signed as the **West Dean Estate** is reached.

Spring

5 Go ahead through the gate and press on ahead to pass through a second gate. At a direction post fork rightwards now on a grassy track that climbs **Haye's Down**. The way is quite steep so take your time and enjoy the fantastic views the open downland offers. Pass through a gate at the top and continue on a well-trodden path through fields to rejoin the **Seven Points** car park. Retrace your outward route over **The Trundle** to the end of this really good walk.

A charming cottage in East Lavant

What to look out for –

Common Whitebeam

Common whitebeam will be seen alongside the track leading to East Lavant and is only found growing on chalk or limestone soils in the south of England. This slow-growing and short-lived striking tree belongs to the same family as the mountain ash and is easily identified during spring because its newly opening leaf-buds are erect and can resemble white magnolia flowers.

The massed white flowers begin to appear in May and are followed by clusters of small fruits that can range in colour from bright red to orange or brown. I have read that a good wine is made from the fruit once it is bletted (when the fleshy fruit is beyond ripe and has started to decay and ferment) but although I am sure it is nice, I think I will stick with the grape for my wine.

2 Wisborough Green and the Wey-South Path

Northlands lift bridge

This splendid field and canal-side route along easily followed paths is a joy during early spring as it passes hedgerows that are weighed down by the massed pure white blooms of blackthorn. After leaving Wisborough Green on a quiet and pleasant country lane, the circuit joins a section of the 36-mile-long Wey-South Path, here tracing the bank of the Wey & Arun Junction Canal that alas, in some places, is no more than a depression in the fields. Passing by New Bridge and what was once a bustling canal wharf, the walk continues through level fields alongside the defunct canal set in a peaceful and scenic landscape. After passing Lording's Lock and Bridge, the way turns north and heads back to the village on a wonderful track that offers easy walking and good views.

Spring

The Facts

Distance 5½ miles.

Terrain Fairly level. The route is not suitable in winter or after heavy rain.

Map OS Explorer 134 Crawley & Horsham.

Starting point The village green at Wisborough Green (GR 049259).

How to get there: Wisborough Green is on the A272, 2½ miles west of Billingshurst. At the centre of the village turn north into Durbans Road and park in a layby beside the village green. If cricket is being played, it is safer to park just past the green in Newpound Lane or School Lane.

Refreshments: The Three Crowns public house in Wisborough Green. ☎ 01403 700239.

Spring

The Walk

1 Go back to the A272 and turn left, passing the **Three Crowns** public house. Keep ahead, pass to the left of the village duck pond and enter the churchyard of **St Peter ad Vincula**. Continue along the left side of the graveyard and at its end go left over a stile. Now turn right along the right-hand side of two fields to meet and cross a stile. Ignore a stile opposite and turn left on a broad path that ends at **Newpound Lane**. Turn right along the lane and continue to its end at a T-junction with the B2133.

2 Cross to the drive opposite signed as a bridleway and continue ahead. When the drive swings right into **Paplands Farm**, continue ahead on a cart track to meet a field gate. Maintain direction ahead, keeping to the left side of a large field to a direction post at its end. Turn right to meet an old canal lock and a bridge. Cross the bridge to join the **Wey-South Path**, turn right and continue along the canal bank until a road is reached at **New Bridge**.

Along the way you will pass Northlands lift bridge, reputedly the only one in the south of England. Although the decking weighs in at 5 tons, the balance is such that it takes only a pull of 45 lbs to raise it.

3 Cross the road and continue on the **Wey-South Path** where you soon pass by a private residence that began life in 1839 as a warehouse on the once bustling **Newbridge Wharf**.

The duck pond at Wisborough Green   13

Spring

Newbridge Wharf was the furthest point inland of the Arun Navigation. In 1813 an extension called the Wey and Arun Junction Canal was cut to connect it to the Wey Navigation at Stonebridge Wharf near Guildford, thus making it possible to barge goods direct from the south coast to the River Thames at Weybridge and on into London. After the canal closed in 1871 it became known as 'London's Lost Route to the Sea'.

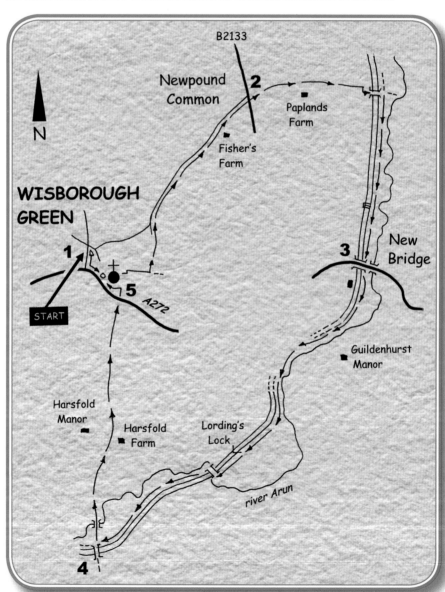

Continue on the well-signed **Wey-South Path** to a pretty picnic spot by **Lording's Lock**. Remain on the path to cross restored **Lording's Bridge** before continuing along the right-hand bank of the canal until a wide crossing track and gates are met.

4 Leave the long-distance path here by turning right along the track signed as a bridleway. Soon follow the track through a large field to reach the buildings of **Harsfold Farm**. Here the track divides and you should keep ahead on the left fork. Press on along a tarmac driveway and follow it until it ends at the A272.

5 Cross the road to **Glebe Way** opposite and in 20 yards fork left on a drive that leads to the church graveyard. Follow a path leftwards and go around the church to rejoin your outward path, where a short stroll past the duck pond and pub brings this walk to an end.

spring

What to look out for –

Blackthorn

It is fair to say that during early spring you will not have to look too hard to spot blackthorn – the blossom is pure white, quite stunning and profuse. Because of blackthorn's habit of throwing up many suckers it generally forms dense thickets which make it pretty much impenetrable to man or beast due to its very sharp thorns.

The glorious spread of flowers first appear in March on bare branches and although an early indicator of spring's arrival, they are sometimes accompanied by bitterly cold weather which gives rise to country folk referring to this occurrence as 'a blackthorn winter'.

Blackthorn is a wild relative of our cultivated plum and the fruit borne from September to November, called a 'sloe', is similar to the plum: blue-black in colour with an attractive bloom. Unlike the plum, however, it is highly astringent, making it virtually inedible, although it does make a tasty jelly and is used in the making of sloe gin.

3 Butler's Copse and Angmering Park

The woodland puts on a spectacular bluebell show in spring

This is a woodland walk with the wow factor! During late April and early May the woodland floor is carpeted by massed bluebells and is a sight to behold. Beginning in Butler's Copse, the way passes through a patchwork of indigenous, well-managed woodland and although bluebells line most of the way, Stonyland Copse has probably one of the best displays. The first turning point comes at Patching Hill where the short grasses of the open downland and the magnificent views make a perfect picnic spot. Returning to woodland, the route passes by Michelgrove Park where the quiet walker has a chance of spotting a roe deer or two as the route continues along wonderful tracks lined by wildflowers.

The Facts

Spring

Distance 5 miles.

Terrain Fairly level. This easy-to-follow route is at its very best in springtime, while during the heat of summer, the woodland offers cool dappled shade. It is best avoided in winter or after prolonged rain due to the sticky clay soil.

Map OS Explorer 121 Arundel and Pulborough.

Starting point Car park in Butler's Copse (GR 061065).

How to get there The car park can only be reached from the east-bound lane of the A27, 2½ miles east of the Littlehampton/Arundel roundabout. The turn off is signed as Dover Lane. Continue to the end of the lane to reach the car park.

Refreshments There are no refreshment facilities on the walk, so why not picnic along the route.

The Walk

❶ From the end of the car park furthest from the entrance, go ahead to meet an estate drive in 15 yards. Turn right along it and when it ends at a T-junction, press on along a signed bridleway. Ignore a crossing track by a gate and continue ahead.

❷ At the end of a field on your left, a junction of bridleways is met. Go left here and in 100 yards turn right on a signed bridleway that passes through **Stonyland Copse**. Now press on ahead and ignore all crossing tracks. After leaving woodland, the route continues through fields on a well-trodden path that leads to a pedestrian gate.

❸ Pass through the gate and turn left alongside a hedgerow to cross the brow of **Patching Hill** where the shade of spreading oaks offers picnic sites aplenty. Later, pass through a second gate, enter woodland and continue along a signed bridleway. Continue ahead, ignoring tracks to left and right, and look out for a bridleway sign on your right that indicates the bridleway *now turns left only.*

❹ From this sign, we leave the bridleway and continue ahead. When the track divides, follow the right fork to meet a forestry road in 50 yards and turn

Spring

The view from Patching Hill

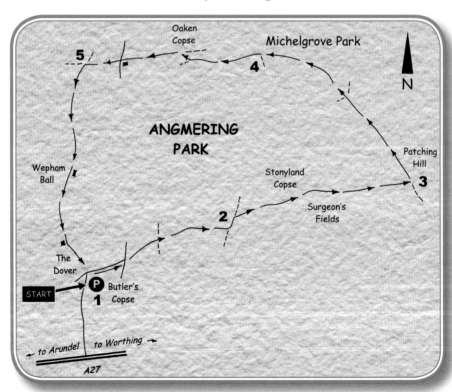

leftwards along it. After passing an isolated house, cross an estate drive and go ahead through a gate. Continue along a tarmac drive signed as a bridleway, to meet a junction of paths at the foot of a dip.

5 Turn left here on a bridleway where the shadier soils support wood spurge and later pass cottages at an area known as **Wepham Ball**. Press on ahead and keep to the left fork when beside an isolated flint house, to soon reach the car park to end this colourful walk.

Spring

What to look out for –

Wood Spurge

A good indicator of ancient woodland is the plants that grow within it: hazel, oak, beech and maple that form the canopy, while below grow bluebells, wood anemone, wood spurge and mosses. It is a sad fact that over the past 80 years, at least half of our ancient woodlands have disappeared either under a plantation of pine, or to the plough and surprisingly few are protected by law.

Wood spurge is the ancestor of many garden varieties of euphorbia and is an odd-looking plant that lacks both petals and sepals. The green cup-like structure of the bracts contains male and female 'flowers' and therefore it can self-pollinate, a handy feature for a plant growing early in the season. As any gardener who has euphorbia knows, if a stem is broken it will bleed a milky latex substance which is toxic and may well cause skin irritation.

4 Rusper and the Sussex Border Path

Walking through a field of rape

This lovely springtime field and woodland walk begins in the fine old village of Rusper. The route starts by following the Sussex Border Path across fields and through Horsegills Wood where the path is lined by swathes of bluebells, primroses, wood anemone and greater stitchwort – a real treat. On reaching the first turning point of the circuit by the handily-placed Royal Oak pub on the outskirts of the village, the way leaves the long-distance path as it crosses Boldings Brook that is lined by massed ransoms. Heading south on easily-followed field paths and pretty farm drives, the route then turns back towards the village where this appealing walk all too soon ends.

Distance 5 miles.

Terrain Fairly level. The route is not suitable during winter or after prolonged rain due to the sticky clay soils.

Map OS Explorer 134 Crawley and Horsham.

Starting point The village car park beside the church in Rusper High Street (GR 205374).

How to get there Rusper is signed off the A264 at Faygate, 3 miles west of Crawley.

Refreshments The Plough & Attic Rooms in Rusper High Street offers burgers, light bites and a good selection of main meals. ☎ 01293 871215.

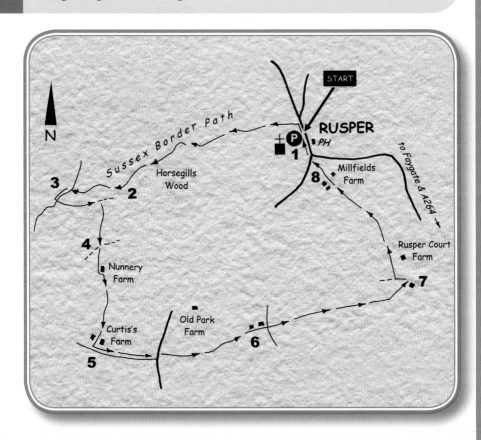

Spring

*The Walk*_____

1 From the car park entrance, go left along the **High Street** to the tennis courts. Turn left here and pass the left side of a football pitch before continuing ahead on the signed **Sussex Border Path** over a field to enter **Horsegills Wood**. Cross a woodland ghyll and climb steps at the far side. Follow the path through a kissing gate and along the left side of a field. Go through a second kissing gate and continue on a path through woodland and across a small brook.

The Sussex Border Path loosely follows the inland boundary of Sussex, once the home of the South Saxons. Beginning on Thorney Island, the path finally ends 159 miles later in Rye.

2 About 15 yards before a brick parapet is reached, follow the signed **Sussex Border Path** rightwards over a stile to enter a field. Go ahead and cross a stile in the hedgerow on your right. Press on along the left field edge and at its end, go through a gate. Pass a barn and continue rightwards along a driveway. In 50 yards cross a stile on your left and continue diagonally right to the corner of the field, beyond a field byre. Cross a stile and continue along the left side of the meadow to reach a country lane.

3 Leave the long-distance path here and turn left along the lane, passing the **Royal Oak** pub. Immediately after the car park, turn left on a signed path and go through the pub garden to cross **Boldings Brook**, where a plethora of ransoms line its banks. Go ahead on a signed path that passes through a bluebell wood. As the woodland ends, go ahead for 35 yards before turning right at a finger post. Pass a waymarker in 60 yards and go ahead along the right-hand side of three oak trees. Press on to a fourth oak and a waymarker beyond.

4 At the field end, pass through a small ghyll, cross a bridge and continue

Spring

The route crosses a pretty ghyll

up steps to meet and cross a stile. Ignore paths left and right and go ahead along the left field edge to join a driveway at **Nunnery Farm**. Follow the drive left and then right and remain on it until it passes **Curtis's Farm** and ends at a country lane.

5 Go left along the lane and when it ends at a T-junction, go left for 20 yards before turning right on a signed, straight path through the centre of a large field. After passing a prominent oak tree on the crest of a low rise, continue ahead towards buildings in the tree line ahead.

6 Pass the buildings and continue ahead passing a barn conversion. Go over a stile by the end of its parking area and press on over a small paddock to meet and cross a lane. Continue ahead following a line of oak trees and remain on this path as it later becomes fenced. Cross two stiles in quick succession to enter a field and continue to a stile to the left of the house at the far side.

7 Turn left along a concrete drive to meet a second drive on your right in 100 yards. Turn right along this drive and at the gateway to **Briar Cottage** fork left on a signed footpath. Follow the right-hand field edge and at its end, go left for 10 yards and cross a stile where the path divides. Follow the left fork through a field before continuing between fences to reach the buildings of **Millfields Farm**.

8 Go ahead on a path along the rear of gardens to a car park and continue along the left side for 30 yards to rejoin the path that ends at a village street beside the **Star** pub. Turn right to the **High Street**, where a left turn soon brings you back to the car park and the end of this walk.

What to look out for –

Ramsons

Along the first half of the route you will see dense patches of ramsons, also known as wild garlic, that grow on the damp shady soil beside the brooks and streams the route passes. Each bulb produces two deep green broad leaves and a triangular flowering stem up to 30 cm high, topped by up to twelve pure white flowers. The leaves emerge in March and the flowers, initially sheathed by bracts, in April and May. Their early season is necessary because they have to complete their flowering cycle before being shaded out by trees.

The leaves are edible and have a mild flavour suitable for a sandwich garnish, a mixed leaf salad or better still, to be shredded and sprinkled over a risotto or pasta dish. They tend to lose their flavour when cooked.

5 Ardingly Reservoir and the Ouse Valley

A tranquil view of Ardingly Reservoir

This wonderful walk through peaceful fields is idyllic on a warm spring day when blackthorn blooms in the hedgerow and sunny banks are studded with primroses. After leaving Ardingly Reservoir, the route follows well-signed field paths alongside the infant River Ouse where the way goes under the Balcombe Ouse Valley Viaduct and later passes Great Bentley Farm to reach its furthest point. A quiet country lane followed by a pretty farm drive leads to more scenic field paths, all with wonderful views. After passing magnificent Stone Hall, the way all too soon ends back at the reservoir.

Spring

The Facts

Distance 4¾ miles.

Terrain Undulating. The route is suitable for most times of the year, though it can be muddy after prolonged rain.

Map OS Explorer 135 Ashdown Forest.

Starting point Coin-operated, pay on entry car park at Ardingly Reservoir (GR 335286).

How to get there Ardingly is on the B2028, 6 miles south-west of East Grinstead. From Ardingly, follow College Road south-west for 1 mile before turning right along the drive to the reservoir.

Refreshments Picnic along the route or at the reservoir picnic area.

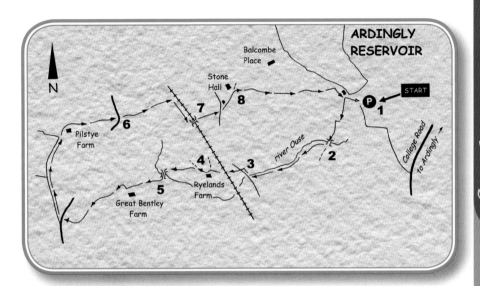

Spring

The Walk

❶ From the car park, go up the slope to **Ardingly Reservoir** and the sailing club. From the slipway, climb a grassy knoll to meet a waymarker and turn left here to pass through a kissing gate in 50 yards and enter a field.

Man-made Ardingly Reservoir was created in 1978 by damming the Shell Brook and the Ardingly Brook.

Follow the left-hand field edge and at its end turn right along its edge to soon enter a second field. Continue along the left edge of this field and at the bottom of a slope cross a footbridge over a stream.

❷ Go ahead over a second footbridge, this time over the infant **River Ouse** –

Walking towards the Ouse Valley Viaduct

during spring the bank of the river here is a mass of ransoms/wild garlic. Ignore a path ahead of you and fork right to follow a grassy path through fields that remains close to the river and finally ends at a road.

3 Turn right alongside the road and soon after passing a cottage turn left over a stile. Cross a field on a well-trodden path that leads under the famous **Balcombe Ouse Valley Viaduct** after which the path soon ends at a farm drive.

4 Turn left along the drive and follow it right, passing pretty **Ryelands Farm**. In 25 yards, fork left by a footpath sign and press on along a field edge to meet and cross two stiles in quick succession. Now continue over a field diagonally half-leftwards to reach its distant corner and cross a stile. Turn right along the next field edge on the well-signed path and re-cross the **River Ouse** via a footbridge ahead of you.

5 Press on ahead along the left-hand field edge and at its end go up steps to meet the drive to **Great Bentley Farm**. Turn right along the drive that has great pastoral views to meet a road at its end. Go diagonally left over the road and turn sharp right into **Cherry Lane**. Continue on this quiet lane until it bends left by the entrance drive to **Pilstye Farm**. Follow the farm drive that soon swings right, passing the farmhouse, and go ahead between barns. The drive continues as a cart track between fields and ends at a road.

6 Cross a stile opposite, continue down a grassy slope and go ahead through trees to soon cross a footbridge on the left. Follow the left side of a field and cross a stile in its corner. Continue along the left side of the next field as it climbs to meet the railway and follow its edge rightwards towards a bridge over the railway line.

7 Cross the bridge and go ahead to a small footbridge and stile in the hedgerow opposite. Turn diagonally half left over the next field and cross a stile to meet a road. Cross the road and continue ahead along a driveway, passing a lovely gatehouse.

8 When opposite impressive **Stone Hall**, go right along a concrete drive where across the field you will see magnificent **Balcombe Place**.

Grade I listed Stone Hall was built in the late 17th century and was originally occupied by the Bray family. Balcombe Place was built in 1865 by John Hankey and during the Second World War became the headquarters of the Women's Land Army. Today it is a nursing home.

When the drive ends at a gate, go through a field gate on your left and maintain your original direction, aiming for the right edge of woodland and a stile. Press on alongside woodland before continuing ahead over the field to meet and cross a stile opposite. Now go half-diagonally left to the bottom corner of this field, pass through a gate and go ahead to cross a stile in 30 yards. Follow the grassy path that soon leads back to the reservoir and the end of this scenic walk.

What to look out for –

Cuckoo pint

Cuckoo pint is a shade lover and is often seen growing where other plants cannot survive. The first spear-shaped green leaves, often with black spots, appear at the beginning of the year and by late spring are followed by a large erect spathe that protects the strange-looking flower. At its base are minute hairs that trap tiny flies attracted to the flower's offensive smell and once trapped, it is not until they have pollinated the plant that these hairs wither and release the unwilling helpers. By September the spathe has gone leaving behind the plant's 9-inch-high fruiting spikes. Each one generally contains some 15 to 25 berries that start off green before eventually changing to a shiny bright red when ripe.

The plant has attracted around one hundred other names, including Jack-in-the-pulpit, parson-in-the-pulpit, wake-robin and lords and ladies to name but a few, and throughout the centuries it has been used in folk medicine for such diverse ailments as the plague and ulcers. The name cuckoo pint is a corruption of two Anglo-Saxon words that indicate our ancestors believed the plant to have aphrodisiac qualities, although I must say here that it is extremely poisonous and must not be handled.

6 Pagham Harbour Nature Reserve and Selsey

Beside Pagham Harbour

This fascinating, level and diverse walk first leads you through the internationally-recognised nature reserve where a pair of binoculars may be of benefit. A raised pathway is easily followed alongside the salt marsh as the route heads towards the sea, passing the 13th-century chapel of St Wilfrid along the way. After reaching the seashore, the walk continues towards the town of Selsey, following the sea wall along the undeveloped seafront. After passing the lifeboat station, the way turns inland and continues along quiet residential roads before turning north down the interesting high street. Leaving the town, the circuit then continues through peaceful arable farmland before ending back at the nature reserve.

The Facts

Distance 7 miles.

Terrain Level.

Map OS Explorer 120 Chichester.

Starting point The car park at Pagham Harbour Nature Reserve (GR 857965).

How to get there The nature reserve is on the B2145 Selsey road, 5 miles south of the A27 at Chichester.

Refreshments Picnic on the beach or visit nearby Selsey where there are plenty of refreshment places.

The Walk

❶ From the opposite side of the car park to the Information Centre, follow a path that passes a Discovery Area. At an open area of marsh, ignore a path on your left and go ahead to pass a sluice before following the path left. This raised path leads you alongside wetlands and gradually swings rightwards where there are distant views to **Pagham** across the reed beds and salt marshes. At one point the path brings you to a shingle beach, but after 80 yards heads inland and ends at the graveyard of **St Wilfrid's Chapel**.

St Wilfrid's Chapel is a fragment of a much larger Norman church that was demolished in 1864. The stained-glass windows include one that depicts the nature reserve.

❷ Go through the centre of the graveyard and exit via the lych-gate to a parking area. Now follow a path leftwards that passes the remains of an earthwork that once supported a Norman fortified stone tower. When the open area of salt marsh is reached, turn right and continue to the shingle seashore.

❸ The way continues rightwards along the top of the shingle bank or, tide dependent, along the seashore. When a variety of seaside cottages are reached, some plainly showing their original purpose, walk on along the rough road that fronts them. At a tarmac road on your right, continue along the sea wall on your left for ¾ mile.

❹ A few yards after passing under the lifeboat station walkway, leave the

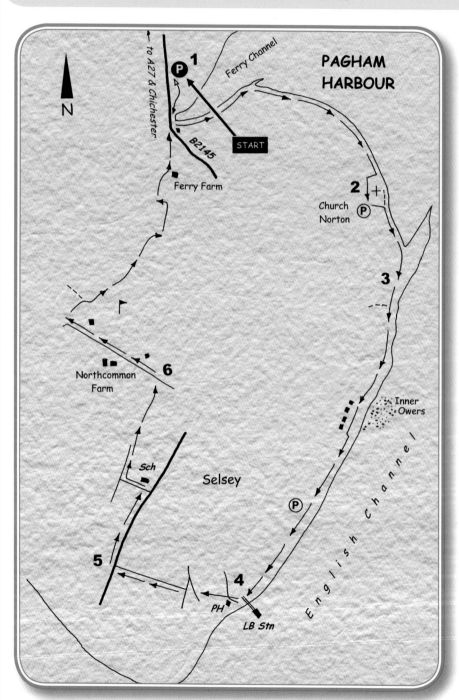

N

to A27 & Chichester

P **1**

Ferry Channel

PAGHAM HARBOUR

START

B2145

Ferry Farm

2
Church Norton
P

3

Inner Owers

Northcommon Farm

6

Selsey

Sch

P

5

English Channel

4

PH

LB Stn

sea wall by turning right along a residential road to meet the **Lifeboat Inn**. Maintain direction ahead here on a path between gardens. Cross a road and press on along the footpath to a second road. Now continue ahead along this residential road until it ends at Selsey's **High Street**.

St Wilfrid's Chapel

Summer

5 Turn right along the **High Street** and finally, as you begin to leave the bustle of the main street behind, pass a Methodist church on the left before turning left along **School Lane**. At the end of the school grounds on your right, turn right along **Paddock Lane** where you pass holiday caravan sites. Keep ahead along a tree-lined track until it ends at a quiet lane.

6 Turn left here and pass the entrances to **Selsey Golf Club** and later **Selsey Country Club**. When the lane finally turns left, go ahead on a footpath to a field. Turn right along the field edge and now remain on the well-signed path, soon ignoring one to the left, until it finally ends at the B2145 Selsey road. Turn left along the road for a few yards before crossing to a footpath to the left of gates to **Ferry Farm House** (*it is safer to walk further away from the bend in the road before crossing and returning to the footpath*). Pass a vehicle barrier to meet up with your outward route, where a left turn returns you to the car park to complete this lovely walk.

What to look out for –

Pagham Harbour Nature Reserve

The reserve is made up of saltmarsh, mudflats, lagoons, reedbeds and shingle beaches that total around 1,500 acres. Although called a harbour, that all ended in 1870 when a dam was built across the harbour mouth and the area was reclaimed for farmland. Thankfully for us, the sea broke through during a storm in 1910 and much of the area became flooded again and has remained so until this day. It is an important wildlife site for waders and wildfowl that include Brent geese and grey heron year round,  while its summer visitors include wheatears, sandwich terns, chiffchaffs and sand martins.

7 Fernhurst and Northpark Copse

Looking towards Telegraph Hill

This scenic field and woodland route leaves Fernhurst on a farm drive that offers spectacular views across the heavily-forested Weald. After walking pretty field paths and woodland trails with a barely perceptible rise of 200 ft, the turning point is reached and the circuit passes through the majestic woodland of Northpark Copse. After an easy descent from this range of hills, the way continues along field paths and farm lanes – all with superb rural views as it returns through this magnificent and remote part of West Sussex. The route is at its very best in late August when a good variety of fungi display themselves.

Distance 5¼ miles.

Terrain The first half of the circuit rises gently by 200 ft with the remainder downhill or level.

Map OS Explorer 133 Haslemere and Petersfield.

Starting point The car park in Cross Field, off Vann Road, Fernhurst (GR 895284).

How to get there Fernhurst is on the A286, 3 miles south of Haslemere. From the crossroads at the centre of the village, go west on Vann Road and in 120 yards turn left into Cross Field.

Refreshments The Red Lion pub east of the crossroads.
☎ 01428 643112.

The Walk

1 From the car park, go back to **Vann Road** and turn left along it to soon meet **Hawksfold Lane East** on the left. Follow this quiet lane and ignore a left fork. At the gate to **Hawksfold Farm**, fork left on a fenced path to soon reach a field. Cross a stile, fork right and cross a second stile at the field end. Continue on a well-signed path through trees and pass the grounds of a large house.

2 At the end of a barn, turn right and pass an extensive garden before continuing left on the signed path to reach and cross a stile. Go ahead along the left field edge and cross a stile at its end. In 10 yards turn right on a bridleway alongside a field and at its end continue on the well-used path through woodland to a T-junction by an ancient boundary stone. Turn left here to soon reach a field and continue along its left edge until a narrow lane is met.

3 Turn right along the lane and at a right bend, go left on the signed path to enter a field and continue along its right-hand edge. Cross a stile at its end and continue on a well-used path alongside a wooded gully. At a crossing cart track, press on ahead on a forestry track, making sure you follow the waymarkers. Soon after the path rises more steeply, you reach a T-junction below **Telegraph Hill**.

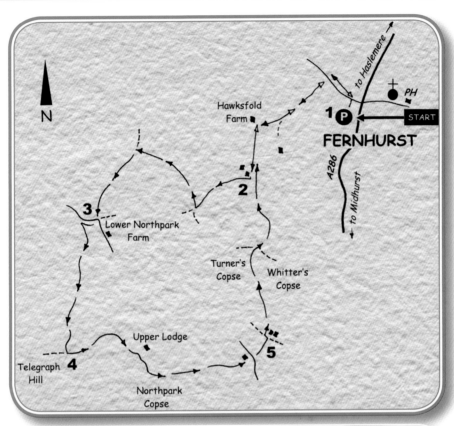

The circuit affords great views over the Weald

Summer

4 Turn left on the signed path and ignore forestry tracks on your left. Keep right at a fork and remain on the curving track to reach the edge of woodland. Cross a paddock with **Upper Lodge** to your left, and continue along its boundary fence. Some 15 yards beyond a garden pond, turn left and continue along the boundary fence to a drive. Press on along the drive to reach a lane and go ahead on the track leading to **Corner** and **Cuckoo cottages**.

5 About 10 yards before the cottages, cross a stile on your left. Turn right, pass the cottages and cross a field on a distinct path before continuing through woodland. Go ahead at a crossing bridleway and soon cross a brook before climbing a short rise to reach a field. Cross the field on a grassy path and pass through a gate at the far end, continuing ahead on a cart track. At a junction of tracks, go ahead along the right side of a field towards the buildings of **Hawksfold Farm** to rejoin your outward path and retrace your steps to complete this enjoyable circuit.

What to look out for –

Pheasant

Many a time along this route a pheasant has flown up from my feet – I don't know who is the most startled, me or it. Pheasants are most frequently seen feeding along the grass verges of country lanes and as the country motorist knows, have absolutely no road sense.

This picture shows a male cock resplendent with its copper-coloured plumage, crescent breast markings and dark green head adorned with bright red wattles. The hen is much less colourful, having mottled buff and black markings and a shorter tail. Pheasants are believed to have been imported into Britain by the Normans during the 11th century and are resident throughout the year, rearing between eight to fourteen chicks that hatch out in April or May.

8 Loxwood and the Wey & Arun Canal

Walking the canal towpath

This easy-to-follow peaceful circuit begins beside the defunct Wey & Arun Canal. Once known as 'London's lost route to the sea', a dedicated band of volunteers are changing that. The route follows the canal bank westward, where their heavy task soon becomes apparent. Continuing through peaceful countryside, the way later swings away from the canal and meets the halfway point as it passes through Alfold Bars not far from the Surrey border. Before long the route follows a scenic path through fields with outstanding views as it makes its return to the canal, from where a short stroll completes this lovely circuit.

Distance 4½ miles.

Terrain Level. A good route for most times of the year but at its best during summer.

Map OS Explorer 134 Crawley and Horsham.

Starting point The public car park beside the Onslow Arms pub, Loxwood (GR 042311).

How to get there Loxwood sits on the B2133, 4 miles north-west of Billingshurst. The Onslow Arms is at the south end of the village.

Refreshments The Onslow Arms, Loxwood. ☎ 01403 752452.

The Walk

1 From the far left end of the car park, climb steps to meet the restored section of the **Wey & Arun Canal**. Turn left and pass the rear of the **Onslow Arms** to reach the B2133. Cross the road diagonally right and continue along the towpath where you will see the work the canal volunteers have ahead of them. Press on along the towpath and ignore paths to your right to eventually pass a house and cross a driveway.

Stepping out on the field path

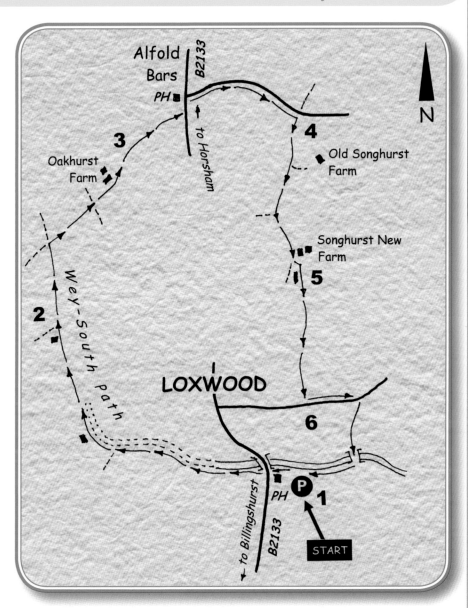

② Continue ahead along a path beside the now indistinct remains of the canal. Pass through a gate and, 120 yards after passing through a second gate, a junction of paths is met. Now turn right along the signed **Sussex Border Path** which later leads you around the right side of **Oakhurst Farm** to meet a quiet lane.

3 Turn right along the lane and follow it until it ends at the B2133. Here turn left to soon meet the **Sir Roger Tichbourne** public house and the halfway point of the circuit. The way continues along **Pigbush Lane** opposite where, after passing a few well-appointed houses, a short rise is climbed to meet paths signed to left and right.

4 Our way is right, on a signed footpath along the drive to **Old Songhurst Farm**. At a sharp left bend, keep ahead on the signed path. At the end of the garden of **New Songhurst Cottage**, bear left and cross a stile in 8 yards.

5 Continue ahead along the right-hand field edge towards a group of barns which you skirt to the left. Pass the rear of a farmhouse and press on along the right-hand side of the field. Keep ahead to finally cross a stile onto a lane.

6 Turn left along the lane and, at a left bend, turn right on a signed bridleway through woodland to rejoin the canal, where you should now turn right along the towpath to complete this walk.

What to look out for –

Banded Damselfly

Banded damselfly can be seen beside almost any canal, river or pond during the summer and autumn months. Skimming just above the surface of the water with a characteristic weak flight, they often settle on the waterside foliage where they lay their tiny eggs.

It is from these eggs that nymphs emerge and they follow a similar life-cycle to their larger cousins, the dragonfly. The nymphs remain underwater and breathe through three flap-like gills in the tail of their body. They stay underwater for up to five years and, being carnivorous, prey on many forms of aquatic life with their pincer-like jaws that make them ferocious hunters. Once fully grown, the nymph climbs out of the water, its skin splits open and the adult damselfly struggles out to live for only a few more weeks before mating, laying eggs and dying.

9 The South Downs Way and Wepham Down

Magnificent Wepham Down

Probably the very best walk in West Sussex because of the outstanding panoramic scenery it passes through and a route that is so easy to follow. The circuit begins with far-reaching views as it follows the South Downs Way long-distance path along the top of the Downs before turning south on a wide track and heading for Lee Farm, nestling in an idyllic downland bowl. Wildflowers line the route, some rare, as the way turns again along an undulating track that leads to wonderful, rolling Wepham Down and its colourful wildflowers. From here the circuit makes its way to the summit of the Downs once again in a barely perceptible climb of 250 ft to rejoin the long-distance path that is followed back to the car park to complete this great walk.

Summer

The Facts

Distance 5¾ miles.

Terrain Undulating downland, with one easy rise of 250 ft.

Starting point Kithurst Hill car park (GR 070124).

How to get there The car park is signed off the B2139, 2 miles east of Amberley, 1 mile west of Storrington. Follow a single track road south to reach the top of the downs and the car park.

Map OS Explorer 121 Arundel and Pulborough.

Refreshments Picnic along the route or there are several eateries in Storrington.

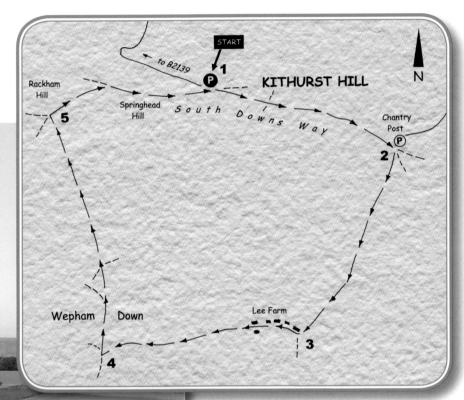

Rackham
Hill

START

1

KITHURST HILL

N

Springhead
Hill

South Downs Way

Chantry
Post

2

5

Wepham | Down

Lee Farm

3

4

to B2139

The Walk

1 From the car park entrance, fork right and pass a gate to meet the **South Downs Way** long-distance path. Turn left along the track and remain on it for 1 mile until you reach a parking area at **Chantry Post**.

2 Turn right here, pass through a gate and continue on a track signed to **Lee Farm**, ignoring a track forking left. Remain on this wonderful track for 1 mile as it gently descends from the heights of the Downs and brings you to the large barns and driveway of **Lee Farm**.

Admiring the view

③ Ignore the drive to your left and go ahead on a drive alongside barns, later passing a couple of houses before continuing between farm buildings. Ignore a left fork and remain ahead on the drive, where a keen eye during June and July may spot a pyramidal orchid or two on the grassy bank (please don't pick or disturb them in any way).

④ After climbing a rise, a junction of tracks is met where the circuit turns right to pass a field gate in 35 yards. Ignore a footpath on your left and continue ahead across **Wepham Down** on a broad track signed as a bridleway. When the track forks left, go ahead through a gate and press on along a narrower bridleway, later ignoring another to your right.

⑤ After a steady but easy climb up the downs, the path ends at a T-junction with a wide track. Turn right here and when this track is later joined from the left by the **South Downs Way** path, turn right along it to return to the car park and complete this amazingly scenic circuit.

What to look out for –

Chicory

At point 4 of the circuit, chicory will be seen growing in the farmland set-a-side margin beside the track. It is a chalk-loving plant that sends up tall grooved stems that during early summer display light blue flower-heads with delicate petals that are toothed at the ends.

Unlike cultivated chicory, or endive as it is also known, the leaves of the wild plant can be bitter to the taste, although the long tap root, similar to a carrot, can be roasted and used as a caffeine-free 'coffee'. Herbalists often recommend the plant for jaundice and spleen problems while the juice of the leaves promotes the production of bile and is believed to eliminate excessive internal mucus. The plant is also useful to soothe inflammation of the skin by a poultice of boiled leaves and flowers wrapped in cloth. Modern research also suggests that chicory may be able to lower the pulse rate and reduce cholesterol.

10 Weir Wood Reservoir and the High Weald

A stunning landscape surrounds Weir Wood Reservoir

This superb route begins at the water's edge where many water birds, some rare, can be spotted from a hide beside the car park. After a short climb, the way follows the High Weald Landscape Trail through tranquil scenery with panoramic views and later passes through the glades of Dunning's Wood that make a great picnic spot. The halfway point comes on the outskirts of East Grinstead, from where the route turns south along a farm drive that provides easy walking and before long the reservoir is rejoined. By following the bank westward, the outward path is met and from here it is an easy stroll back to the nature reserve.

47

Summer

The Facts

Distance 5½ miles.

Terrain Hilly to begin with but generally level after that. The walk is at its best during summertime but suitable for other seasons, too.

Map OS Explorer 135 Ashdown Forest.

Starting point Car park at Weir Wood Reservoir Nature Reserve (GR 383341).

How to get there Weir Wood Reservoir is south of East Grinstead. From the town, go south on Dunning's Road that later becomes West Hoathly Road and in 2½ miles turn left into Legsheath Lane where the car park and nature reserve will be found on the left in ¼ mile.

Refreshments: There are plenty of picnic spots along the way, or visit the Old Mill pub at the halfway point. ☎ 01342 326341.

The Walk

1 From the hide at the end of the car park, follow a path through trees to meet **Legsheath Lane** and continue rightwards along it to the junction with **West Hoathly Road**. Turn right along the road and press on uphill. At a sharp left bend, turn right along a small drive and continue until gates are met.

2 Turn left here on the signed **West Sussex Border Path**, later ignoring a path on your left by power cables. When the path turns parallel with the reservoir, go left over a stile in 75 yards to join the **High Weald Landscape Trail**. Continue along the right side of a rising field and pass under power cables to gates on your right. Ignore them and press on ahead on an uphill path through trees to a T-junction.

3 Turn right and continue uphill. Cross a stile on your right and follow a path between banks. As you leave the trees, a junction of paths is met with **Standen** seen on your right. Press on ahead along the right-hand field edge and pass through a tree line at the top of the hill.

4 Turn right on a well-trodden path, with panoramic views across the **High Weald** and, at the driveway to **Standen**, turn left along it to its junction with a road. Go left along the road for 60 yards before turning right on a bridleway.

A glade in Dunning's Wood

Summer

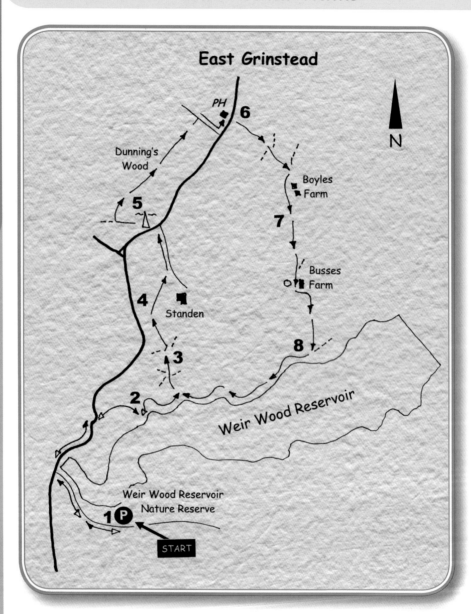

In 25 yards follow it leftwards to meet a playing field. Continue along the right side of this field and when around halfway, turn right on a signed path.

5 Follow this path through **Dunning's Wood** and its magnificent glades that make the perfect picnic spot. When the path ends at a small residential road, go ahead to a T-junction and turn right to soon meet **Dunning's Road**, where a left turn brings you to the **Old Mill** pub and the halfway point of the circuit.

6 Turn right on a path opposite the pub and walk through **Sunnyside Recreation Ground**. Pass a barrier at the far end and follow a well-trodden path with a brook on your left. Ignore paths to left and right, and cross a bridge over the brook. In 8 yards turn right and continue through woodland with the brook now on your right to meet a drive. Turn right along the drive and pass the pristine buildings of **Boyles Farm**.

7 Continue on the drive to reach **Busses Farm** where the **West Sussex Border Path** is joined. Keep ahead between a pond and farm buildings, at the end of which you should turn left and go through the field gate ahead of you to follow a bridleway.

8 At a T-junction, turn right on the well-defined path that skirts the reservoir to rejoin the outward route, from where you retrace your steps to complete this walk.

Summer

What to look out for –

Great Crested Grebe

From the hide at the end of the car park there is the chance to observe water birds undetected and if you are lucky enough you may spot a great crested grebe or two. As the name implies, it is the largest of our grebes and if you are even luckier, during springtime you may witness their weird head-shaking and weed-exchanging courtship display.

Their summer plumage includes black frills on each side of the head that can be extended during courtship but are lost during the winter months. Their clutch of eggs, usually three or four, are laid in March or April within a nest made of rotting vegetation floating on the water surface but always anchored to aquatic plants.

11 Cocking, the South Downs Way and Heyshott Down

The panoramic view from the South Downs Way

This stimulating downland and village route is simple to follow and beginning on Cocking Hill, the way rises fairly easily through stunning scenery to meet with the heights of Heyshott Down some 730 ft above sea level. From here there is a steep descent through the peace and tranquillity of woodland and a nature reserve to reach the fields below. After following a quiet cart track that leads to Cocking, the way passes through the village and soon begins its return up Cocking Hill on a cart track that is none too difficult for a person of average fitness. This is a good walk for most times of the year but is especially colourful during autumn.

Distance 4½ miles.

Terrain Hilly, with one steep descent.

Map OS Explorer 120 Chichester, South Harting and Selsey.

Starting point Cocking Hill car park (GR 875167).

How to get there Cocking sits on the A286, 3 miles south of Midhurst. The car park is off the A286, ½ mile south of the village.

Refreshments There are none on the route so picnic along the way.

The Walk

1 From the car park, cross the A286 and continue along a farm track signed as the **South Downs Way**. When **Manor Farm** is reached, ignore a byway to your left and continue ahead between a couple of farm houses. Press on uphill on the wide track with magnificent views as it crosses **Manorfarm Down**.

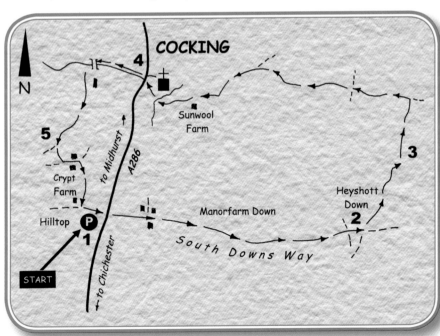

Autumn

In the village of Cocking

2 At the top of the hill ignore footpaths signed to left and right and go ahead to meet a junction of paths in 80 yards. Turn left here through a pedestrian gate and cross the field diagonally half right to pass through a second gate. The way now continues through **Heyshott Chalk Downland Nature Reserve** on a downhill path lined by yew trees.

The lumps and bumps you see here are the old spoil heaps from disused chalk pits that the downland grasses have recolonised. Now protected as a Site of Special Scientific Interest, the area supports lime-loving flora such as bee orchids and horseshoe vetch which are a good source of nectar for insects, particularly bumble bees.

3 At the foot of the slope, continue on a wide grassy cart track between fields with panoramic northerly views. At a T-junction with another track, turn left and now follow this lovely cart track for 1¼ miles, ignoring the occasional paths and tracks to left and right. Soon after passing **Sunwool Farm**, the track bends right, crosses a stream and passes **St Catherine's church** to end at the A286.

4 Turn left alongside the A286 for 15 yards before turning right into **Bell Lane** beside the **Bluebell Inn**. Press on along the lane, pass the entrance to **Old Station House** and go under a railway bridge. In 40 yards turn left along a restricted byway where you will see the defunct railway station that makes a fine residence; even the platform has been retained.

Cocking railway station, now a private house, served the village from 1881. The line ran from Midhurst to Chichester and although passenger services ceased in 1935, freight continued until the line finally closed in 1953.

5 Keep to the restricted byway and when it forks, take the left, less well used byway to reach a T-junction by the well kept buildings of **Crypt Farm**. Turn left here, pass between the buildings and continue on the restricted byway that is signed to the **South Downs Way**. Just beyond a couple of estate cottages the long-distance path is met and here a left turn soon returns you to the car park and the end of this picturesque circuit.

What to look out for –

Spindle tree

Although called a tree it barely reaches 6 metres tall and its delicate greenish-white flowers are insignificant. The spindle tree's preferred habitat is generally in hedgerows and on woodland edges and it often goes unnoticed until autumn comes when its vivid four-lobed magenta fruit capsules appear and split open to expose orange arils that surround the seed.

The wood of the tree is close-textured and was used for making skewers, knitting needles, toothpicks and spindles for the looms of our textile industry.

All parts of the tree are poisonous and there have been reported cases of poisoning that involve children who have been tempted by the vividly coloured fruit so remember, not all fruit from the hedgerow is good for you!

Autumn

12 Benbow Pond and Cowdray Park

Majestic Cowdray Park

This outstanding walk through archetypal Sussex countryside has everything you could ask for: scenic rolling parkland, quiet drove roads, forestry tracks, wildlife and wonderful views. Beginning beside Benbow Pond that supports a good variety of waterfowl, the way goes through peaceful parkland before crossing a golf course and passing a quiet hamlet from where it continues along Wick Lane, now little more than a cart track. Turning north, the route follows a forestry track where there is every chance to spot deer and rises easily to its highest point. As the circuit begins its return it follows level tracks to reach Vining Farm, from where the homeward leg drops gently back to the parkland and Benbow Pond. Great for any time of the year but especially good for the autumnal colours and the lack of mud.

The Facts

Distance 5¼ miles.

Terrain The first 2½ miles rises gently by 350 ft.

Map OS Explorer 133 Haslemere and Petersfield.

Starting point The car park beside Benbow Pond in Cowdray Park (GR 914222).

How to get there Benbow Pond is off the A272, 2 miles east of Midhurst.

Refreshments: Picnic beside Benbow Pond or along the route. There are also several eateries in Midhurst.

The Walk

❶ With your back to the road, walk away from **Benbow Pond** on a track and in 80 yards when it bends right, continue ahead on a grassy path. In 120 yards when a fence ahead is reached, turn left alongside it to meet a kissing gate on your right.

Here, across the meadow on your right, is the Queen Elizabeth Oak, a veteran believed to be 800 years old; Queen Elizabeth I is said to have sheltered beneath it on a visit to Midhurst in 1591.

❷ Do not go through the gate but fork left on a rising path along an avenue of trees. Later ignore a path signed to your left and press on ahead to reach a golf course at the crest of the rise. The way continues ahead and is well signed but watch out for flying golf balls.

❸ After crossing the golf course, go down a slope and continue through a kissing gate. Go ahead over the field and cross a stile beside a gate. Go ahead to the hedgerow, bear left alongside it and pass through a gate to a quiet lane.

❹ Turn right along the lane and when beside **Holly Cottage**, fork left on a small lane. This is traffic-free **Wick Lane**. When the lane bends sharply right ignore a path on your left and continue on the lane. The surface gradually deteriorates and at a bend a junction of paths and tracks are met. Go leftwards here to finally reach a reservoir on your left.

Autumn

5 At the far end of the reservoir, turn right on a forestry track that is soon joined by another from the left. Continue ahead on this track that is occasionally signed by red arrows. The quiet rambler has a good chance of spotting wildlife along here; the last time I came this way I saw two roe deer. After ¾ mile the slowly rising track rises more steeply to meet a directional sign on the crest of the hill. Turn right as directed and follow the forestry track until it meets with a road.

6 Turn right along the road to reach a T-junction. Go ahead now on a bridleway ignoring a track forking right. After passing through woodland, the bridleway continues ahead along the side of a large field. At the field end by **Grevatts Farm**, ignore paths signed to left and right and continue ahead on the bridleway along a cart track.

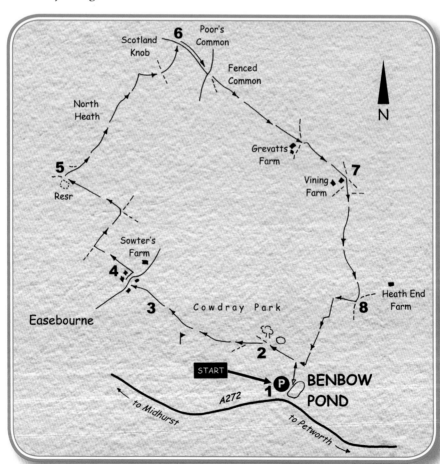

The Queen Elizabeth oak

7 Some 60 yards after passing under power cables at a junction of tracks, turn right on a narrower bridleway and soon ignore a footpath on your right. Pass the entrance gate to **Upper Vining** and in 25 yards ignore a signed path on your left. Continue ahead on the sunken bridleway for ½ mile until a broad track joins it from the left.

8 Our way bends right here to meet a footpath on the right in 45 yards. Go right along a field edge and at the far corner follow the edge leftwards. After a bend in the field edge, cross a stile on your right and maintain your original direction along the left side of this field. In the bottom corner of the field pass through a kissing gate, turn right alongside the fence to soon meet your outward path where **Benbow Pond** and the end of this circuit is just a short distance to your left

What to look out for –

Mistletoe

As you pass along an avenue of trees in point 2 of the circuit, you will notice a good crop of mistletoe above you. The plant is a parasite that lives by extracting a part of its host's nutrients. Every part of mistletoe is poisonous although that hasn't stopped it being used for centuries in herbal medicine for the treatment of epilepsy and asthma.

The plant has two methods of germination and both are by birds, especially thrushes – hence mistle-thrush. The berries bearing the seed are sticky and when eaten, the seed often applies itself to their beaks which they then wipe off on branches of nearby trees, while the second method is via their droppings containing seeds that are deposited on a branch.

Although mistletoe has become a part of our Christmas celebrations, its tradition goes back much further than Christianity. Kissing under the mistletoe is a well-known ancient fertility rite but less well-known is that a berry must be removed for each kiss, and when they have gone, the privilege ceases.

13 The Clayton windmills and the Chattri Memorial

Jill, the 19th-century post mill

This invigorating downland walk leads you through some of the best scenery in southern England – no wonder the South Downs have been made a National Park; the views are quite stunning. Beginning high on the Downs, this figure-of-eight circuit makes its way to Lower Standean where it follows a lovely driveway for 2 miles through stunning scenery to meet the turning point. As the way heads back it passes the Chattri Memorial, an unusual sight amidst the rolling downland landscape. The route continues to climb gently through this breathtaking panorama as it follows the Sussex Border Path to meet the South Downs Way path on the crest of the Downs, where a downhill path leads back to the car park. A lovely autumnal walk but suitable for any time of the year.

Autumn

The Facts

Distance 6¾ miles.

Terrain Undulating.

Map OS Explorer 122 Brighton and Hove.

Starting point The car park beside the Clayton windmills (GR 302134).

How to get there The windmills are signed off the A273, a third of a mile south of Clayton which is 1 mile south of Hassocks.

Refreshments The Jack and Jill pub in Clayton. ☎ 01273 843595

The Walk

❶ From the car park entrance, go left and pass the **Jack and Jill windmills** on a stony track.

Jack is a five-storey brick tower mill built in 1866 to replace an earlier mill and is now a private residence. Jill is a wooden post mill built in 1821 and more correctly called Lashmar's New Mill. It is open to the public on several days during the summer. The names Jack and Jill are believed to have originated from day trippers to Brighton during the 1920s.

When the track divides, fork right and soon pass between farm buildings. Press on ahead and ignore a crossing track in 80 yards. Continue ahead on the well-trodden path beside a golf course.

❷ At a T-junction, turn left to reach a tree-line and pass through a gate on your right. Follow the path

to a second gate and go leftwards through it. Now follow the right-hand field edge and ignore a gate on your right on the crest of a rise. Continue downhill alongside the field edge and follow it leftwards to meet a gate.

3 Turn right through this gate and continue downhill on a cart track that brings you to an eclectic collection of farm buildings at **Lower Standean**. Continue ahead on the now tarmac-surfaced driveway and remain on it for the next 2 miles as it follows the valley floor.

4 About 30 yards before the driveway ends at a T-junction, turn sharp right through a gate almost going back on yourself and follow an indistinct grassy path through the centre of a rising field. Soon the top of an electricity pylon

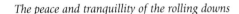

The peace and tranquillity of the rolling downs

Autumn

Autumn

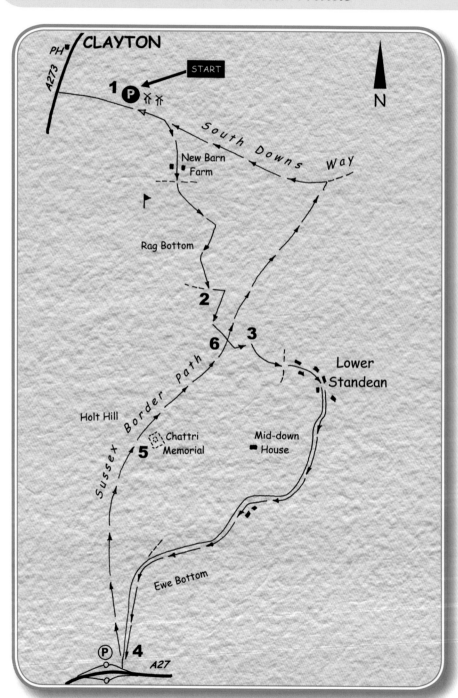

CLAYTON

PH

A273

START

1 P

South Downs Way

New Barn Farm

N

Rag Bottom

2

6 3

Lower Standean

Holt Hill

Sussex Border Path

Chattri Memorial

5

Mid-down House

Ewe Bottom

P 4

A27

comes into view and you should aim for that and pass through a gate beside it. Continue ahead on the grassy path that you can see bending rightwards in the distance.

5 At a second gate the way continues ahead, but before that you may wish to explore the **Chattri Memorial** down the slope to your right. The route continues on a well-defined path that brings you to a gate and your outward route.

6 Press on ahead along an indistinct grassy path, pass through another gate in the distance and continue ahead until a T-junction is met with the **South Downs Way** path. Turn left and follow this stony track downhill for ¾ mile to reach the car park and the end of this great circuit.

Autumn

What to look out for –

The Chattri Memorial

The route passes close to the Chattri Memorial which was built to honour all the Indian soldiers who died during the First World War. Many sick and injured Indian soldiers were treated in Brighton hospitals and sadly not all survived. To respect their religious or caste beliefs, different funeral arrangements were set in place; Muslim dead were sent by road to the Shah Jahan Mosque in Woking, Surrey, where an Imam officiated before their burial nearby.

By tradition, Hindus, Sikhs and Ghurkhas were cremated and their ashes scattered, so this site was created for that purpose. The granite slabs forming part of the memorial are placed directly over the original cremation platforms. An annual service is held here on the third Sunday in June. A chattri, or 'chhatri' is a dome-shaped pavilion in Indian architecture and is a popular embellishment on their buildings.

14 *Cowfold and Little Parkminster*

Autumn

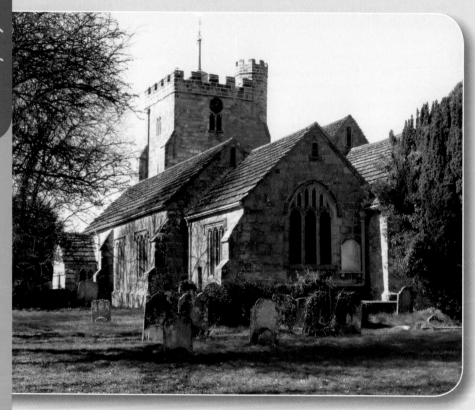

St Peter's church at the start of the walk

This lovely pastoral walk through fields to the south of Cowfold begins in the centre of the village beside ancient St Peter's church. Easy walking is the order of the day on well-signed paths across level fields with extensive views. With the tower of St Peter's now in the distance, the route heads towards St Hugh's Charterhouse, a Carthusian monastery at Little Parkminster. Pressing on through idyllic scenery, the way continues along field paths and farm drives to return to the village recreation ground and the end of the circuit. I chose to walk this route in autumn because of the fantastic colours of the trees, but spring and summer would be equally good.

Distance 4½ miles.

Terrain Level. Not suitable after prolonged rain because of the sticky Wealden clay.

Map OS Explorer 134 Crawley and Horsham.

Starting point The car park by Cowfold recreation ground (GR 215225).

How to get there Cowfold is at the crossroads of the A272 and A281, 3 miles west of Bolney. The car park is off the A272 at the centre of the village.

Refreshments The Hare and Hounds ¼ mile south of the village on A281.
☎ 01403 865354

The Walk

❶ From the car park, go to the crossroads with the tower of **St Peter's** beyond. Pass to the right of the village store and enter the churchyard. Continue along the right side of the church and follow its rear wall left before continuing on a signed fenced path. Pass the side of the village school and follow the field edge leftwards. Keep to the well-trodden path as it turns right over a brook and follows the right-hand side of a field. Cross a stile and continue ahead along a field edge, passing to the left of a small pond.

❷ At the corner of this field turn left along its edge and cross a stile ahead of you. Immediately after passing **Gervaise Cottage**, turn right over a stile and press on alongside the house and field edge. In 120 yards cross a brook to reach a directional sign and from there go diagonally left to another sign and stile in the distance.

❸ Cross the stile; turn left and pass through a tree line in 35 yards. Now turn immediately right and follow the tree line and field edge. Towards the end of the field go diagonally left to cross a stream and go ahead and pass through a kissing gate opposite. Now continue ahead through two paddocks to reach a country lane.

❹ Turn left along the lane and ignore a path on your right at **Clockhouse**

Farm. Near the top of a rise, turn left on a signed bridleway alongside a field fence. Ignore a footpath signed left and continue ahead to meet and pass through a field gate. Now turn right and cross the field aiming for the left edge of woodland and a finger post.

By now you will have noticed the buildings of St Hugh's Charterhouse, especially its spire that stands over 200 ft tall. Founded in 1873, it is the only post-Reformation Carthusian monastery in Britain and is unusual in that the Great Cloister which connects 34 hermitages to the church is over ½ mile long, making it one of the longest in the world.

5 Cross a stile and turn left along the field edge to its corner before turning right to meet and cross a stile. Ignore a path on your left and press on ahead to a distant stile and finger post beyond an oak tree. Cross the stile and continue ahead, aiming to the right of a distant house.

6 Pass the house and turn left on a grassy track that passes its frontage to soon meet a cart track. Continue right along the track and when it soon bends right, fork left on a less well-used track and follow it until it ends at a road in **Little Parkminster**.

The golden glow of autumn in the fields

Autumn

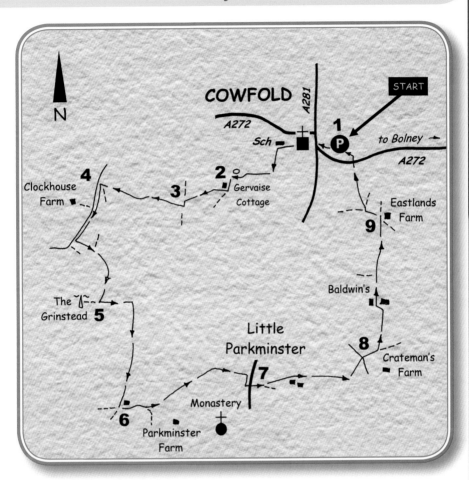

7 Turn right along the road and in 60 yards go left along the drive to **Gratwicke**. Cross a stile on your left in 50 yards and go diagonally right through a field, aiming to the left of a wooden building. Pass the rear of this building and a house before continuing along a field edge. Press on alongside a second field but as you enter a third, fork left across it and go over a stile at the far side.

8 Go over a driveway and continue ahead on a fenced path. Cross a stile in the hedgerow on your left and continue over a field towards a large barn. Pass through a hedgerow at the far side and turn left to cross a stile and meet a farm track by a house. Turn right along the track that soon becomes surfaced and remain on it to meet a fork besides a wonderfully created barn conversion.

9 Fork left here and in 130 yards turn right on a signed path and when it forks in 15 yards, follow the left fork through woodland. Cross a stream on your left and continue alongside gardens to reach a small road. Go ahead here to soon reach the A272. Cross to a gate diagonally left and continue through the recreation ground to reach the car park and the end of this fine walk.

What to look out for –

Parasol Mushroom

No, the Martians haven't landed! This unusual looking object is a young parasol mushroom. After pushing up through the soil, the immature cap is egg-shaped and covered in a pattern of scales that look like snakeskin. As it matures the cap breaks away from the stipe (stalk) leaving a fleshy ring behind. As it further matures the cap opens to its fullest and is almost flat and stippled with upturned scales. When fully grown, this fairly

common mushroom of fields and paddocks is one of the largest in Britain and grows up to 40 centimetres high with a cap some 25 centimetres in diameter.

All mushrooms and toadstools you see above ground are only the flowering part of the main fungi body, the mycelium, which is a thread-like structure that remains underground. Just as in flowers, these blooms are for the purpose of reproduction, but rather than having seeds, they produce spores that are so tiny that just one mushroom can release many millions.

15 Henfield, the Downs Link Path and the River Adur

The sun's rays lighting up the path

This splendid track and riverside walk has the minimum of instruction and is extremely easy to follow. Leaving Henfield behind on the broad Downs Link Path, the way heads north to meet its first turning point where Betley Bridge crosses the River Adur. Here the circuit turns south and for 3 miles follows a wide grassy path alongside the river that meanders through scenic meadows with the magnificent South Downs as a backdrop. Rejoining the Downs Link Path by Stretham Manor, the way turns north and an easy stroll back to the village follows. Although I walked this circuit during early autumn, it is eminently suitable for any time of the year.

Autumn

The Facts

Distance 5¾ miles.

Terrain Level.

Map OS Explorer 122 Brighton and Hove.

Starting point The car park in Upper Station Road, Henfield (GR 205163).

How to get there Henfield is on the A281 4 miles west of Hurstpierpoint. From the centre of Henfield opposite the White Hart pub, go west along Church Road and continue along Upper Station Road to the car park beside the Cat and Canary public house.

Refreshments The Cat and Canary pub beside the car park. ☎ 01273 492509

The Walk

1 From the car park, head away from the road on the signed **Downs Link Path.**

2 After 1 mile and with **Betley Bridge** 100 yards ahead, you come to a small bridge lined by railings. Turn left here on a signed path to meet the **River Adur** and continue leftwards along its bank. Now follow the river bank for 3 miles and ignore two footbridges along the way.

This eastern section of the Adur rises at Ditchling Common in East Sussex and along the way is joined by the western Adur that rises in Slinfold. Together they continue to the English Channel 3 miles away at Shoreham-by-Sea.

3 After rounding a bend in the river a third and larger bridge carrying the **Downs Link Path** is met by **Stretham Manor**. Turn left here along the old track bed ignoring side paths until finally, the track ends at a residential road.

The Downs Link Path was created in 1984 with the aim of providing a 30-mile link between the North and South Downs for walkers, horse riders and cyclists. Much of the route follows two dismantled railways, the Steyning Line and the Cranleigh Line, both closed in the 1960s during Dr Beeching's infamous cuts. The small modern housing estate in Station Road is on the site of Henfield station and is ironically called 'Beechings'.

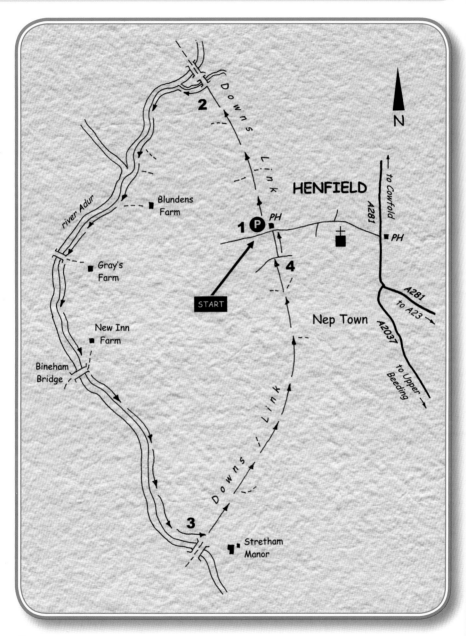

4 Turn right here and then left into **Station Road** after 30 yards. Ahead of you the **Cat and Canary** pub will be seen, where a few steps leftwards bring you to the car park and the end of this circuit.

Autumn

The River Adur

What to look out for –

Common Teasel

Along the route are patches of common teasel which is a biennial, meaning that for its first year it only grows roots and a rosette of leaves. By the following spring or summer, the stem of the plant shoots up, generally to about 3 ft high and flowers from several flowering heads which open successively from the centre, both upwards and downwards.

The plant's common name of 'teasel' comes from its once cultivated close relative Fuller's teasel that at one time was grown in large quantities for the woollen industry, where the dried seed heads (shown above) were used to 'tease' out the nap of the cloth.

This striking plant is also known as 'Venus' basin' because the rainwater that collects in the first year's rosette of leaves was, many years ago, thought to be beneficial as an eye wash and as a cure for warts.

Harting Downs, the South Downs Way and Hooksway

A marker post in Bramshott Bottom

This wonderfully scenic downland route in my opinion is one of the very best in the newly created South Downs National Park. Beginning on Harting Downs where there are extensive panoramic views on offer, the route soon passes through the peace and tranquillity of Bramshott Bottom as for a while it follows the South Downs Way path. After leaving the long-distance path the way passes Hooksway, a tiny isolated hamlet where the inviting Royal Oak pub and its large garden sits in the beautiful setting. Continuing along a track through woodland to the circuit's furthest point, the way begins its return by rejoining the well-signed South Downs Way path. This walk is wonderful at any time of the year but is especially good during winter because it is mud free.

Winter

The Facts

Distance 7¼ miles.

Terrain Quite hilly but not beyond the ability of a person of average fitness.

Map OS Explorer 120 Chichester, South Harting and Selsey.

Starting point National Trust Harting Downs pay and display car park (GR 790181).

How to get there South Harting is 12 miles north of Chichester. Go south from the village and soon turn left along the B2141 to the car park on the left at the top of the hill.

Refreshments The Royal Oak pub at Hooksway. ☎ 01243 535257

The Walk

1 With your back to the road and the escarpment to your left, cross a large grassy area and soon pass through a pedestrian gate. Continue ahead on the well-defined grassy bridleway with fine views over **South Harting** below. As you pass through a dip ignore paths to left and right and press on ahead. At the end of a thicket, follow the path leftwards and through a gate. Continue downhill; pass through a second gate and go ahead to meet a cairn and fingerpost in **Bramshott Bottom**.

2 Turn right here on a path that climbs gradually out of the valley and is signed as the **South Downs Way**. At the top of the rise, continue along a field edge and at its end ignore the **South Downs Way** path on your left. Keep ahead here to soon pass the grounds of **Telegraph House** and continue along its drive.

3 At a right bend in the tree-lined drive, continue ahead on a bridleway between fields. At a marker post, ignore a footpath signed to the right and turn left, keeping to the bridleway that eventually ends at a small country lane. Turn left along the lane to meet the **Royal Oak** pub in the hamlet of **Hooksway**.

4 The way continues ahead here; ignore paths to left and right and in 20 yards at a fork, take the right fork signed as a restricted byway. After climbing through woodland a junction of tracks is met by a

Approaching the Royal Oak pub at Hooksway

Winter

Winter

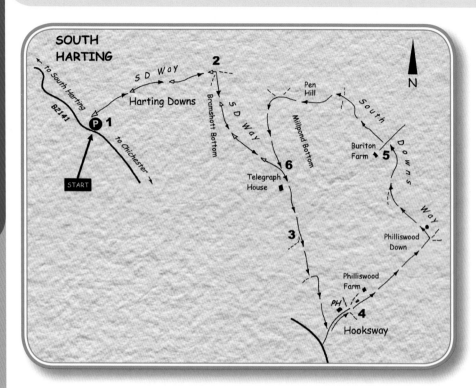

finger post. Now rejoin the **South Downs Way** path by turning left here along a wide cart track.

Very soon a small monument to Joseph Oestermann will be seen on your right. He died on 13th August 1940, the first day of the Battle of Britain when his Junkers Ju 88A-1 was shot down by an RAF squadron of Hurricanes from nearby Tangmere whilst on a sortie to attack Farnborough. His comrades were fortunate enough to bale out and were captured but the young captain was killed when his plane crashed here and exploded. It is good to see that the monument is still well tended.

Remain on this good track, later ignoring a left fork, to meet its end at a T-junction with a farm drive.

5 Follow the well-signed **South Downs Way** path leftwards and then right in 30 yards. The long-distance path is very well signed and you should remain on it as it crosses **Pen Hill** before sweeping leftwards and passing alongside a very large field.

6 At the field end, the way rejoins the outward route and here you should turn sharp right and follow the **South Downs Way** path back into **Bramshott Bottom** to meet the cairn and marker post. The way turns left here and crosses **Harting Downs** to rejoin the car park to bring this exceedingly good, energetic walk to an end.

What to look out for –

Lichen

Lichens are small and because there are around 1,500 species in Britain can be hard to identify and are generally broken down into three divisions: crustose lichens are those forming a crust-like growth; foliose lichens form a leafy growth; while fruticose lichens have a shrub-like appearance.

Lichen grows on exposed branches of bushes and trees, as here along the route, walls, gravestones and even roof tiles; anywhere where it can receive good sunlight and be left undisturbed. Lichen is a combination of two different organisms, a fungus and an alga, neither part living independently of each other and both known by the name of the lichen – the dominant partner.

Almost all lichen are asexual meaning they are both male and female and when they cast their spores on the breeze, each spore will need to find its correct algal partner for it to germinate and begin a new life that in some cases may last for up to 100 years. Pictured here is a close-up view of *Xanthoria polycarpa* from the foliose family.

17 Eartham Wood, Stane Street and Great Down

Walking along Stane Street

This really good winter walk through indigenous woodland lets you stretch your legs 'out of season' no matter what the weather. The route begins by following Stane Street, a rare surviving Roman road that leads you easily through Eartham Wood where there is every chance of spotting wild deer. After leaving the old trackway behind, the route climbs Upwaltham Hill on a not too difficult track to reach its highest point from where there is level walking to reach Gumber Corner. Turning south, the way follows a wonderful cart track across Great Down to the fields below before returning through Eartham Wood on an undulating track. A great circuit for any time of the year but it is especially good during winter because of the lack of mud.

The Facts

Winter

Distance 6 miles.

Terrain Some hills.

Map: OS Explorer 121 Arundel and Pulborough.

Starting point The car park and picnic site in Eartham Wood (GR 939106).

How to get there Eartham is signed off the A27 west of Fontwell. The car park is ¾ mile north of the village.

Refreshments The George Inn at Eartham. ☎ 01243 814340

The Walk

❶ From the car park entrance turn left along the road to soon reach a bend. Go left here on a broad stony track and in 40 yards fork right on a narrower

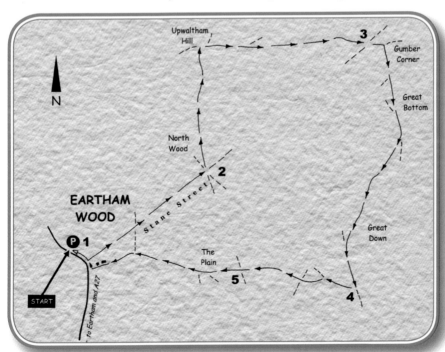

Winter

The view after leaving the woodland at point 2 of the walk

track known as **Stane Street**. There is an information plaque near here that gives the history of this Roman road. Keep ahead along this wonderful track until you reach a large junction of tracks by a seat and finger post. The last time I came this way a herd of fallow deer, if seven constitutes a herd, crossed the track ahead of me with three bucks showing an impressive display of horns.

2 Turn left here on a rising track signed to **Upwaltham**. Ignore side paths and keep to the main track until it ends at a T-junction. Turn right, in 25 yards ignore a left turn and keep ahead to soon exit woodland and maintain your direction on a well-trodden cart track signed as a bridleway. When a junction of bridleways is met, go ahead on the bridleway signed to **Gumber Bothy**.

3 At the end of the field on your left, ignore paths to left and right and continue ahead through a small tract of woodland to meet a wide cart track at an area known as **Gumber Corner**. Turn right on this track that offers panoramic views over **Great Bottom**. When the track swings sharply right, keep ahead on a narrower track that follows a field edge. At a fork by a marker post, keep to the right fork and continue through woodland. The track later follows a field edge with **Great Down** to your left and becomes narrower before finally ending at a wide rutted farm track and a finger post.

4 Turn right along the farm track signed as a bridleway and when it forks at the edge of woodland, follow the left fork. At the end of woodland, ignore a crossing path and go ahead on the bridleway between fields to reach **Eartham Wood**.

5 Continue ahead for 1 mile on this well-defined bridleway and ignore occasional side paths. As you exit woodland, pass a couple of forestry buildings to meet a road. Turn right along the road to soon reach the car park and the end of this really enjoyable walk.

What to look out for –

Common Dog Violet

Clumps of the common dog violet grow by the side of the path at point 2 of the walk and although most wildflower books will tell you their flowering season begins in April, here along the sunny woodland edge they can flower as early as February. Some violets are named after the habitat in which they grow, as in the case of the fen and marsh violets, while three others contain the suffix 'dog': the common dog violet, the heath dog violet and the wood dog violet. The 'dog' element simply means the flower contains no scent, an indication that our ancestors regarded it as only 'suitable for dogs'.

   A more intriguing fact is that they produce what are called 'cleistogamous flowers' – simply meaning that some flowers do not actually open for pollination but are able to self fertilise. Because there is little wind on the woodland floor, violets in common with a few other plants hurl their seeds from their capsules by an explosive mechanism which gives them a chance of spreading away from the mother plant, while ants sometimes distribute them further.

18 Southwater, the Downs Link Path and Marlpost Wood

On the Downs Link Path

This classic Wealden circuit is perfect for a bright frosty day when there is a crunch underfoot and stillness to the air. Beginning beside Southwater Country Park, the route soon leaves the housing of the village behind as it follows the Downs Link Path through lovely scenery to Two Mile Ash. Turning south on a quiet road to join wonderful woodland, the way meets an old drove road and passes ancient Crookhorn Farm to reach magnificent Marlpost Wood and a good forestry track. Winter is the best time to spot a buzzard or two here as they soar above the canopy of the forest whilst making their distinctive call. After leaving woodland, it is just a short walk to the country park and a path that passes the lake and visitor centre. The 70 acre country park is on the site of an old brickworks and is made up of three lakes surrounded by grassland with seats – the perfect picnic spot. The walk is equally as good during other seasons.

The Facts

Distance 5 miles.

Terrain Fairly level. Not suitable after prolonged rain due to the sticky clay soils.

Map OS Explorer 134 Crawley and Horsham.

Starting point The car park in Southwater Country Park (GR 161259).

How to get there The car park is off Cripplegate Lane and signed from a roundabout on the A24 south of the village.

Refreshments The Visitor Centre café is open on Fridays, weekends and school holidays. There are seats around the lake suitable for picnics.

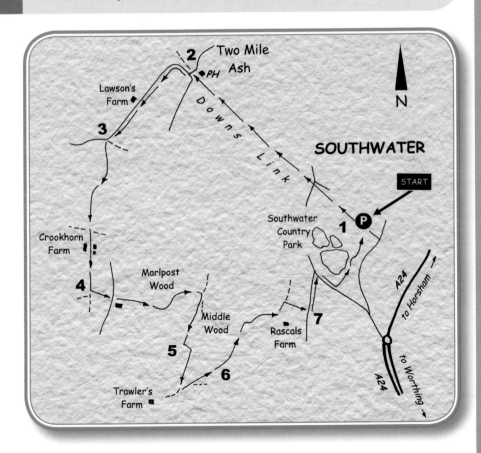

The Walk

1 From opposite the car park entrance, go up a slope to the top of the old railway embankment and continue rightwards along the well-used **Downs Link Path**. When the path meets the **Village Surgery** and a road junction; cross the road and press on under a bridge opposite to soon meet and cross a field. Ignore a bridleway on your left at the far side and continue ahead along the **Downs Link Path** for ¾ mile.

Medieval Crookhorn Farm, passed on the route

2 Some 35 yards before a road bridge is reached and beside the large garden of the **Bax Castle** public house, go left up a slope to meet a road. Turn right alongside it, go ahead over a road junction and continue along **Two Mile Ash Road** where later you pass Grade II listed, 17th-century **Lawson's Farmhouse** with its wonderful Horsham slab roof.

3 When trees encroach on either side and the road bends right, two bridleways are met on your left. Ignore the one signed left and follow the one that continues ahead, rises gently between low banks and leads you through lovely woodland. After emerging from woodland the bridleway continues along an old drove road lined by trees. Ignore side paths and keep ahead passing between the buildings of medieval **Crookhorn Farm** and its duck pond. Maintain your original direction along the drove road to a wide crossing track.

4 Go left here on a signed public bridleway to soon cross a country lane. Press on ahead along a cart track, passing the frontage of a large house. The track continues through **Marlpost Wood** and a shallow valley where it crosses a stream. On the upward slope at a T-junction, the way is rightwards. Soon ignore a bridleway signed to your left and when the track divides in 60 yards, follow the right fork to reach the woodland edge and a field.

5 Pass through a gate, turn left along the field edge and at its corner follow the edge rightwards. Before the field end, pass through a second gate and continue ahead to a track and finger post in 65 yards. Turn left here along the track and when it soon bends right, go ahead through woodland on a signed footpath.

6 At the woodland end, pass through a gate, turn left, cross a field and continue on a grassy path through a plantation of poplar trees. Turn right at the end of the plantation and at its end go through a gate on your left. Go ahead and in 120 yards by a finger post, turn right on the signed path and soon continue along a field edge to meet a track where a left turn brings you to a residential road.

7 Turn left along the road and continue to its end to a road junction. Go ahead to a footpath opposite and turn right to an entrance to **Southwater Country Park**. Go left under a height barrier and follow a path signed to the visitor centre. At a road 15 yards to your right, turn sharp left to meet the shore of the lake. Turn right now to pass the visitor centre and the **Southwater Watersports Centre** buildings to rejoin the car park and bring this walk to an end.

What to look out for –

Coot

Once back at Southwater Country Park look out for coot that can sometimes blend in with accompanying ducks, although their smaller heads and white frontal shields make them easier to identify. They are aggressive little birds and can often be seen chasing others of their kind by 'scuttering' across the surface of the water on their long,

greenish legs. They feed mainly on weed from below the surface of the water and can stay submerged for up to 30 seconds.

The nest is quite large for the size of bird and is constructed of aquatic vegetation. The eggs, anywhere from four to nine, are stone-coloured with brown specks and are laid from April onwards. The coot is a British resident throughout the year.

19 Bramber, the Monarch's Way and Truleigh Hill

St Mary's House, where Charles I is said to have sheltered

This energetic and spectacular route follows the Monarch's Way long-distance path along the quaint village streets of Bramber and Upper Beeding before making a climb up the north flank of the downs. Here the South Downs Way path is joined for a short distance and with breathtaking panoramic views continues on a gentle rise to reach its highest point on the crest of Truleigh Hill some 650 ft above sea level. The route then heads south before rejoining the Monarch's Way path with distant views to the sea. After skirting Beeding Hill the way makes an easy descent to the River Adur where level paths lead back to Bramber. Although suitable for any time of the year it is especially enjoyable on a crisp, clear winter's day.

Distance 6¾ miles.

Terrain There is one notable rise of 310 ft that should not trouble a person of average fitness and a further gradual rise of 300 ft to reach the highest point of the circuit.

Map OS Explorer 122 Brighton and Hove.

Starting point The car park in the centre of Bramber village (GR 187106).

How to get there Bramber is off the A283, 3 miles north of the A27 at Kingston by Sea.

Refreshments There are several pubs in Bramber and Upper Beeding.

The Walk

1 With your back to the car park entrance and **Bramber Castle** 200 yards to your right, go left along the village street that forms a section of the **Monarch's Way** long-distance path. Pass historic **St Mary's House** where King Charles II is believed to have sheltered after his defeat at Worcester. Cross the **River Adur** and press on through **Upper Beeding,** keeping ahead at a mini roundabout. At a second roundabout opposite the **Rising Sun** public house, turn left along a short stretch of the A2037.

The Monarch's Way is a 615-mile long-distance path that follows closely the route King Charles II is believed to have taken during his escape after his defeat at the Battle of Worcester in 1651.

2 After passing the **Towers School** and the end of **Manor Road**, turn right at a bend on the signed **Monarch's Way** path that is initially lined by houses. Soon the track becomes steeper; take your time here and your efforts will be finely rewarded by spectacular views. The track ends at a small car parking area by a lane.

3 Fork left along the lane that is shared by the **South Downs Way** long-distance path and, with stunning views, the route continues to climb a hardly noticeable further 300 ft to pass **Tottington Barn** youth hostel below the crest of **Truleigh Hill**.

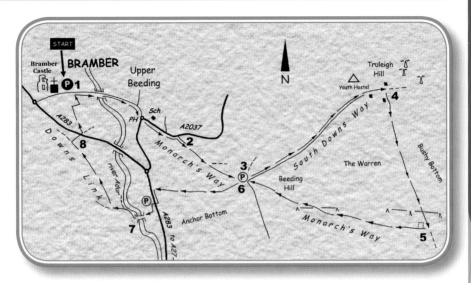

4 Continue ahead, pass the entrance of **Truleigh House** and 100 yards later go right on a wide bridleway. Pass farm buildings and **Freshcombe Lodge** and remain on this scenic track until after passing under power lines an old stock kraal (cattle enclosure) is met.

5 Turn right here on the **Monarch's Way** as it passes through a fold in the

The view over Bramber

Winter

downs. Continue through a gate on the upward slope and go ahead with a fence to your right. Pass under power cables and through a second gate to finally rejoin the small parking area met earlier.

6 Go through a gate to the left of the parking area and follow a grassy track downhill. Soon the way becomes fenced and descends easily to the A283. Turn left along the A283 for 100 yards before crossing to a parking area. Halfway along the parking area go right on the signed **South Downs Way** path.

7 Cross a bridge over the **River Adur** and turn right along its bank. In 250 yards the path forks and the way is leftwards away from the river. When the path soon divides, go right along the signed **Downs Link Path** beside a field.

8 At the field end, follow the path right and leave the **Downs Link Path** by going ahead to meet the A283. Cross the road and a stile to enter a field, fork left and aim for the left edge of a mobile home park. At the far side continue rightwards alongside the perimeter hedge to join its driveway. Go ahead along the drive to meet the village street in **Bramber** where a short distance leftwards brings you to the car park and the end of this invigorating walk.

What to look out for –

Bramber Castle

Originally 'Brymmburh' from the Saxon for fortified place, Bramber Castle was constructed by William De Braose in 1070 along with the close-by Norman church which served as its chapel. The motte and bailey castle is built on a natural mound but sadly little remains today; just one wall of the keep and small sections of the perimeter wall.

The castle's early history is shrouded in mystery but it is known that in 1642 during the Civil War, Parliamentary troops set up guns in the transept of the church to gain a better vantage point from which to batter the castle into submission. The church, seen here in the bottom right of the picture, suffered severe damage during the assault but nothing compared to that of the castle which was largely destroyed.

20 Mannings Heath and St Leonard's Forest

The forestry track at the start of the route

This lovely woodland circuit begins by following a wonderful forestry track alongside Inholms Gill, where a woodland stream tumbles between banks lined by pine trees, and arrives at an area of forest that abounds in legend and is known as Mick Mill's Race. The way continues through majestic woodland before turning and passing a small hamlet to Grouse Road, a quiet country lane. After enjoying pastoral views for ¾ mile the way turns through pretty Frenchbridge Gill to rejoin the outward path, where an easy stroll brings this good circuit to an end. Although suitable for any time of the year, it is especially good in winter as for most of the way it is virtually mud-free.

Distance 4¼ miles.

Terrain Undulating.

Map OS Explorer 134 Crawley and Horsham.

Starting point Roosthole Forestry Commission car park (GR 208298).

How to get there Mannings Heath is on the A281 between Cowfold and Horsham. At the southern end of the village follow Church Road signed to Mannings Heath Golf Club. Later it becomes Golding Lane and finally ends at a T-junction with Hammerpond Road. Turn left here to find the car park on your right in 250 yards.

Refreshments There are none on the route but plenty of picnic spots in the forest.

The Walk

❶ From the car park, follow a wide hard surfaced forestry track for ½ mile to reach a T-junction. Turn left, pass a junction of tracks known as **Mick's Cross** and continue along the **High Weald Landscape Trail**. This straight track is known as **Mick Mill's Race**.

There are differing stories of how this track gained its name. One is that a local smuggler of that name was told by the Devil that he had come to collect his soul. Mick struck a deal that involved racing him through the forest with the winner claiming Mick's soul. Mick won! Another and more likely version is that a Michael Mills planted a long avenue of trees here in 1720.

❷ In ½ mile, when the **High Weald Landscape Trail** is signed to the left, turn right and soon ignore a small path forking right. Continue down a slope to meet a T-junction.

❸ Turn left here and in 100 yards go right on a signed footpath, ignoring a forestry track 20 yards beyond it. Now follow this path and soon pass to the right of **Old Springfield Stud**. Cross a stile and continue along the left side of a field to cross a second stile. Follow an indistinct grassy path rightwards, cross a footbridge over a brook and continue through woodland on the well-trodden path. Keep ahead, later continuing along a cart track to meet a tarmac drive.

4 Cross the drive and soon pass through a field gate ahead of you. Now go ahead along the left field edge to cross a stile and meet **Grouse Road**, a quiet country lane. Turn right along this lane and follow it for ¾ mile enjoying the wonderful pastoral views it offers.

5 About 120 yards after woodland begins on your right, turn right on a well signed public footpath through **Old Copse**. The path leads you down into pretty **Frenchbridge Gill** where you cross a bridge over a stream and continue up the far side to meet a T-junction.

6 Turn left here to meet **Mick's Cross** in 40 yards and your outward path. Turn left again and then right in 30 yards and now make your way back along the hard surfaced forestry track you walked earlier to return to the car park.

Winter

Walking along Mick Mill's Race

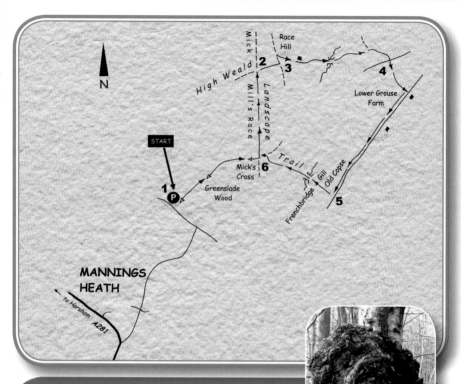

What to look out for –

Birch Burr

After crossing the stream in Frenchbridge Gill in point 5 of the circuit you may notice a silver birch tree on your left with a huge burr on its trunk – quite the largest I have seen on a birch. A burr, bur or burl in American English, is an overgrowth of the tree's own grain that looks rather like a large wart. Differing theories abound regarding the cause of this deformed growth; some believe it is due to damage caused by deer or fencing while another train of thought is that it is because of an insect infestation.

Burrs can occur on almost any species of tree and are highly prized by wood turners or sculptors, while furniture makers use their sometimes spectacular veneers in their trade.